superstars!
superstars!
superstars!

CREATIVE EDUCATION SPORTS SUPERSTARS

fran

robi

k

nson

by Larry Batson

illustrated by
Harold Henriksen

Amecus Street
Mankato, Minnesota 56001

Published by Amecus Street, 123 South Broad Street, P. O. Box 113, Mankato, Minnesota 56001

Printed in the United States.
Distributed by Childrens Press, 1224 West Van Buren Street, Chicago, Illinois 60607
Library of Congress Numbers: 74-4488 ISBN: 0-87191-349-6
Cover: Sports Illustrated photo by Neil Leifer © Time, Inc.
Library of Congress Cataloging in Publication Data
Batson, Larry, 1930- Frank Robinson.
(Superstars)
SUMMARY: A biography of the baseball star whose batting style causes
him frequently to be hit by pitches but has also won him the Triple Crown.
1. Robinson, Frank, 1935- — Juvenile literature. 2. Baseball — Juvenile literature.
(1. Robinson, Frank, 1935- 2. Baseball — Biography)
I. Henriksen, Harold, illus. II. Title.
GV865.R59B37 796.357'092'4 (B) (92) 74-4488 ISBN 0-87191-349-6

frank robinson

Frank Robinson is a menacing sight as he waits for a pitch. His poised bat is motionless. Great ropes of muscle writhe in his forearms as he adjusts his grip. His head and arms jut forward over the edge of home plate into an area ballplayers call "Concussion Alley."

Robinson is hit by pitches more often than any other major league player, but he refuses to back away. He will not give a pitcher an advantage. If one of them tries to shave the outside corner with a curve ball, Robinson wants to be able to hit it solidly.

On this day Robinson's team, the Cincinnati Reds, and the Milwaukee Braves are playing a double-header. The first game is tied in the late innings. Robby wants to get on base, of course; and, if possible, he wants to get into scoring position.

The pitch is outside; but because he crowds the plate, Robinson can reach it. He drives it down the right field line back against the stands. As he runs to first, he can see that the right fielder won't be able to throw him out at second. The first baseman is running out to take the outfielder's throw and relay it. If he hesitates or makes a poor throw, Robinson can reach third base.

He decides to gamble. He rounds second without slackening speed and slides hard into third, a fraction of a second ahead of the throw. The force of his slide knocks Eddie Mathews, the Braves' third baseman, down. "Safe," the umpire signals. Angrily, Mathews slams the ball into Robinson's face and calls him a name. Both jump to their feet and begin fighting.

Mathews weighs 30 pounds more than Robinson. He is one of baseball's strongest men and a skilled boxer. He bloodies Robinson's nose and blackens one eye, which immediately puffs shut. Robinson does little damage, and he jams a thumb when he hits Mathews' head. The fight is broken up, and Robinson has to be helped from the field. Mathews doesn't have a scratch on him.

Even though he can barely see from one eye and can't grip a bat properly with that swollen thumb, Robinson insists on playing the second game. When it is over, he astonishes his teammates by saying, "I won that fight."

"Figure it up," he explains. "I was safe on the play. In the second game I had a homer and a double, drove in one run, scored another, and made a catch that robbed Mathews of an extra-base hit. We won the game 4-0. I won the fight."

That explanation sums up the character and philosophy of Robinson. He is a flaming competitor, by all odds the most aggressive superstar in major league baseball. He has driven himself to stardom in both the National and the American Leagues and has led his teams to championships in both.

He is the only man ever to win the Most Valuable Player award in both leagues. He is also one of 11 players in the history of the game to win the Triple Crown — that is, lead his league in batting average, home runs, and runs-batted-in during the same season.

Robinson is a throw back to the era of Ty Cobb, with whom he has often been compared. To Robinson, a player in another team's uniform is an enemy. On the field, Robinson never has a friendly word for an opponent. The feeling is mutual.

"I hated his lousy guts," Hank Foiles, a catcher for Pittsburgh, once said. Other infielders said even worse things. One reason is that Robinson is a terror on the basepaths. "If you can't break up a double play, knock the man down anyway," Robinson said once. "Make him think a little next time you come around.

But there is another side to Robinson's personality — the one his teammates, friends and family see.

Robinson is a thoughtful man, generous with help and advice. He is a very funny man. He can break up the whole team with one of his sly cracks. He is also so fiercely dedicated to the game of baseball that he will not permit slackness in a teammate. When one of them goofs off, Robinson's sharp tongue jerks him back into line.

Above all, Robinson is a leader — by example on the field, by force of personality off it.

But Frank was not always a leader. As a skinny, bashful boy, he kept his eyes on the ground and pretended not to hear his classmates' greetings at school in Oakland, California, because he didn't know how to make conversation. The young Robinson was so homesick on his first baseball trip, a journey to an American Legion tournament, that he suffered severe stomach pains.

Frank grew up in Oakland and has always made California his off-season home. However, he was born in Beaumont, Texas, on August 31, 1935. He was the youngest of 10 children. His parents separated when Frank was a baby; and he was brought up by his mother, who moved to Oakland when Frank was 4 years old. She still lives there.

Of the neighborhood in which he grew up, Frank wrote in his book, *Baseball Is My Life:* "It was in a rough, mixed neighborhood, mostly Negroes, but also Mexicans and a lot of Orientals. It wasn't a bad, Harlem-type ghetto . . ."

Many of the neighborhood young people did belong to gangs and played, fought, stole, gambled and drank together. Frank never joined one. He was always a loner, shy and slow to make friends. The big reason he didn't join a gang was that running around with a gang would take time away from baseball; and Frank thought nothing was as important as playing baseball.

Baseball was played on asphalt-covered playgrounds in Oakland. "All those years growing up, I don't remember ever eating a hot meal at night," Frank once said. "I'd play till I couldn't see the baseball, then come home. My supper would be cold in a pot on the stove.

"I played every kind of baseball you could think of . . . with broomhandles for bats and golf balls, tennis balls and rolled-up rags for balls. I'd get to the playground early on Saturdays because we had these leagues which played schedules. I'd play in as many games as they would let me, sometimes 3 or 4 in a day.

"I'd slide on those hard playgrounds and tear my pants and scrape skin off, but I didn't care."

Frank played thousands of playground games but never received any expert coaching until he was nearly 15. Then he met George Powles.

Powles, a calm, soft-spoken white man, has a quiet dignity and honesty that appeals to boys. As baseball and basketball coach at McClymonds High School in Oakland, he has coached dozens of athletes who

became college and professional players. At the time he met Frank, Powles was encouraging a skinny, awkward boy named Bill Russell to keep practicing basketball. Two years later, with Russell at center and Frank as a high scoring guard, the McClymonds team won the Northern California championship. Russell went on to stardom at San Francisco University and with the Boston Celtics.

At 15, Frank had reached his full height of 6 feet 1 inch. He weighed about 170 pounds. Frank's legs were, and still are, skinny. Kids on the playgrounds nicknamed him "Pencils."

Powles showed Frank some exercises to increase his strength. "From that day on, that boy shook the house down doing those silly exercises," Frank's mother once said.

Robinson still does them. He still looks slender, too, though he weighs about 190 pounds. But when he strips off his uniform shirt, he reveals impressive ridges of muscle running along his shoulders and down his back. His forearms and upper arms are layered with long, smooth, striking muscles.

Besides the high school team, Powles put Frank on the American Legion team he coached. Frank was a substitute outfielder before becoming a regular. That team won 2 straight national Legion championships.

Frank hit .424 his senior year in high school, and 2 major league teams offered him contracts and a bonus of $3,500. He chose Cincinnati over the Chicago White Sox because the Reds would start him in a higher league — Class C instead of Class D — and at a higher salary — $400 a month instead of $125.

Frank gave his bonus check to his mother and reported to the Reds' team in Ogden, Utah, to begin his professional career. He was just 17 years old, and he had an important lesson to learn: It wouldn't be enough to survive competition on the field. To become a major leaguer, he would also have to overcome loneliness and racial prejudice off the field.

Ogden was strictly segregated. Frank couldn't even attend the movies, always his favorite recreation. White players lived with local families, but Frank and Chico Terry, the only other black player, had to stay in a hotel.

Frank spent 3 seasons in the minor leagues, all in cities that were racially segregated. During those years he made the decision to keep his baseball career and the battle for civil rights and racial equality separate.

While growing up in Oakland, Robinson wrote in his book, "I was never aware of any outright discrimination. I just never thought about it. And I think that that came from my family — my mother, my sisters, my brothers. I never heard any of them say "that white man" or "this colored man." There was just never that type of talk around the house. And I never faced a situation where I was put down because I was Negro."

Robinson is a proud, dignified, and sensitive man with a hot temper he has learned to control. He supports civil rights programs as a private person, not as an athlete.

"I don't think a baseball field or a clubhouse is the place to discuss those things," he says. "A lot of people get mad at me for saying that, but they took the same stand when they were playing. I think it's come to the point where baseball men look at what you can do rather than your color," Frank has said.

One of his friends at Baltimore was third baseman Brooks Robinson, a white Southerner. Visitors to the clubhouse often confused the two, calling Frank "Brooks" and vice versa. Frank would pretend to be bewildered. "Can't understand it," he would say, shaking his head solemnly. "We wear different numbers."

But it was years before Robinson felt comfortable enough to joke in the clubhouse. In the minor leagues and during his first few seasons in Cincinnati, he was at ease only when playing baseball.

Frank batted .348 at Ogden and hit 17 home runs. But the statistic that impressed baseball people most was that he drove in 83 runs in just 72 games. Then and always after, Robby was most dangerous when men were on base.

The next year, Frank was sent to Tulsa, Oklahoma, where he was told to play second base. He was also told to change his batting style to eliminate a hitch in his swing. Both experiments were disasters.

Robinson is a gifted outfielder. He judges fly

balls perfectly, often turning his back at the sound of the bat and running straight to the spot where the ball can be caught. He is a fast runner, though not a very quick starter. He has a strong, accurate arm and can rifle the ball from the deepest part of the outfield on a low, flat arc. But none of these gifts is especially useful to an infielder.

Frank was a terrible second baseman, and the experiment was abandoned after 8 games. So was the attempt to change his batting style.

Frank is a natural power hitter, with great "leverage," as baseball people say. It is a matter of timing as well as strength.

His bat meets the ball just at the instant that he coordinates all the power of his hips, back, and shoulders with a snap of his enormously strong, quick wrists. When that happens, the ball "jumps" off the bat so fast the eye doesn't pick it up until it's almost out of the infield.

He holds his hands high as he awaits a pitch and drops them as he starts to swing. That is called a "hitch". It is a bad habit for most hitters because it throws their swing out of line. But Robinson's wrists are so strong that he can control his swing right up to the point of contact. His hitch just increases his power. When the Tulsa manager made Frank shorten and flatten his batting stroke, he still hit the ball — but all his hits were singles.

The Reds moved Frank from Tulsa to Columbia, South Carolina, after a couple of weeks and put him back in the outfield. He quickly regained his batting eye and hit .336 with 25 home runs while driving in 110 runs. He also scored 112 runs, best in the league.

After his second season at Columbia, Robinson was invited to spring training by the Cincinnati team. A few days before the season opened he was put on the roster; and on April 17, 1956, he played in his first major league game.

Robby hit the first pitch thrown to him off the left-field fence for a double, a couple of feet short of a home run. The second time up he singled. Then in the seventh inning, with the score tied, he was walked intentionally — an extraordinary compliment to pay a rookie.

Frank was the National League Rookie of the Year that season (batting .290 with 38 homers). The next year, he defied baseball's sophomore jinx, raised his average to .322 and was named Sophomore of the

CINCINNATI
25

Year. When he wasn't winning games with his bat, he was doing it with his glove or as a base runner.

"If there is a way to win a key game," said Birdie Tebbetts, then the Reds' manager, "Robby will find it."

Robinson's batting stance is typical of his approach to the game. He didn't crowd the plate in the minor leagues; but when he came up to the Reds, he looked for a competitive edge.

"I knew that major league pitchers, with their fine control, would be able to throw breaking pitches over the outside corner," Robinson said. "I couldn't afford to give them any part of the plate, so I crowded it."

Robinson can hit outside pitches from his stance, even pull them sometimes. But he has paid for it. Over the years he has been hit by pitches more often than any other player.

He led the National League in being hit by pitches in 6 of his 10 years at Cincinnati. When his aggressive baserunning made enemies, pitchers began throwing at him for that, too.

In 1958, a pitch struck Robinson just under the left ear. He dropped as if he had been shot.

"I tried to go to him," said Vada Pinson, a teammate and Robinson's closest friend in baseball, "but my legs wouldn't carry me. I was afraid he was dead."

Robinson woke up in a hospital with a throbbing headache and blurred vision. He rested a few days then insisted on playing.

He discovered that he was afraid!

"In that first month, the fear was agonizing," Robinson wrote later. "I didn't feel it sitting on the bench waiting to hit or stepping into the batter's box. It came on me subconsciously when the pitch was on its way to the plate. I'd flinch and roll back on my heels on the breaking balls."

A batter can roll back like that and still hit a fast ball because it is coming in a straight line. But there is no way that he can hit curves. Word went around the league like lightning, and Robinson seldom saw a fast ball. At mid-season he was batting .240 with 8 home runs and 23 runs batted in.

Robinson decided on a drastic cure, a test of willpower and courage. He resolved to try to hit every pitch to right field, no matter where it was pitched. When a right-handed hitter does that, he has to delay his swing, stand there longer than if he were trying to pull the ball. Robinson tried it in an exhibition game. He batted 4 times and hit the ball to the right each time, twice for safe hits.

Then came the crucial test — an official game at San Francisco against Al Worthington, a curve-ball pitcher. Robinson came to bat in the second inning. Worthington's pitch was a sweeping curve. Robinson waited for it, met it solidly, and drove it over the left-field fence for a home run.

He never again rocked back from a good pitch. He had conquered his fear for all time.

Three years later, he had to overcome another problem, this one the result of a mistake off the field. As his baseball salary increased, Robinson acquired expensive tastes in clothes and cars. "I changed cars like other people did shirts," he said once. "I remember trading one after 5 months."

He carried large sums of money and did all the foolish things that young men who have never had money are likely to do when they get a lot of it. Then he did something really foolish — he bought a gun and began carrying it.

"It was a dumb, kid thing to do," he says now. "I don't think I could ever have used it. I only shot it at the Cincinnati police range with some officers I knew."

One night in February 1961, Robinson was arrested for pulling the gun on a restaurant cook he thought had threatened him with a knife. He spent the night in jail doing some serious thinking.

Much later, when he knew it wouldn't be mistaken as a plea for sympathy, Robinson revealed that he spent most of that night thinking of how that arrest would look to baseball fans. "I especially thought about the kids and what I owed them," he said. "I'd never really faced up to my responsibilities before."

Robinson kept quiet and took his punishment that season. While opponents sang "Lay That Pistol Down" from their dugout or asked umpires to frisk

him for weapons, Robby led the Reds to their first National League championship since 1940. He hit .323, drove in 124 runs, scored 117 runs, and hammered 37 home runs. He won game after game with his hitting, fielding or base-running.

The 1961 championship was the only one the Reds won while Robinson played with them. They came close several times. Twice they stayed in the race until the last week of the season.

Robinson was named Most Valuable Player of the National League after the 1961 season. In 1966 he won the award again — with Baltimore of the American league. He is the only player to be so honored in both leagues.

When he traded Robinson to Baltimore after

the 1965 season, Cincinnati Reds' President Bill Dewitt told angry fans that Robby was "an old 30" who couldn't play at top speed any more.

Robinson promptly made that statement look ridiculous. He became the Orioles' field leader and led them to the 1966 American League pennant and to a World Series victory over the Los Angeles Dodgers. The Orioles took the Series in 4 straight games.

Robinson won the triple crown that year, 1966. His batting average of .316, 49 home runs, and 122 runs batted in led the league. He also led the league in runs scored, 122.

Frank likewise demonstrated to American League crowds that he was one of the game's finest defensive outfielders. Early in the season, he won a game from New York with a leaping catch in front of the right-field fence at Yankee Stadium. As he caught the ball, Robinson tumbled backward over the 4-foot fence into the seats. An umpire had run out and saw the catch clearly, but Yankee Manager Ralph Houk protested the game. Houk argued that nobody could have made the catch and held the ball.

A month later, Robinson made an almost identical catch in Yankee Stadium, again taking victory away from the Yankees. This time Houk did not protest. Robby had made a believer of him.

Robby was as aggressive as ever on the field. When he thought it was necessary, he was also quick to point out a teammate's mistakes. But the Baltimore players also discovered that inside the clubhouse, he was a relaxed, funny man who can take a ribbing and dish it out.

Teammates called him "Tape" because of the yards of it he used to cover various injuries. They claimed that without it, he would fall apart in sections. They picked up "Pencils" and kidded him about his skinny legs. "Without those big feet, you'd sink right into the ground," first baseman Boog Powell would yell.

Curt Blefary, a young outfielder and a good hitter, had trouble catching the ball. Robby nicknamed him "Clank," allegedly for the sound the ball made bouncing off his glove. Once when the team's bus stalled in traffic beside a huge pile of scrap metal in a junkyard, Robby suggested that Blefary hop off and look for a new glove.

The Orioles had never finished higher than third before Robinson joined them. After he arrived, they won 4 pennants in 6 seasons. Baltimore captured first place in 1966. They won 3 pennants in a row from 1969 to 1971. The Orioles were a collection of fine players before Robby joined them. He pulled them together into a team.

Once Baltimore Manager Earl Weaver nodded toward him and said: "There is the guy. Maybe we'd win it without him and maybe we wouldn't. But he makes it easy."

Many baseball people believe that Baltimore would have won 6 straight pennants if Robinson hadn't suffered an injury that hampered him for 2 seasons.

In 1967, he slid into Chicago second baseman Al Weis while breaking up a double play. Weis had to have surgery on his leg and missed the rest of the season. Robinson sat on the bench for six weeks "babying a busted skull," as he put it. He suffered from chronic headaches and had double vision in his right eye through the 1968 season. His depth perception was faulty. Sometimes he didn't see a pitch at all.

Robinson's vision cleared up in 1969, and he went on to have 3 of his finest seasons. He batted .308, .306, and .281 as the Orioles won pennants each year. In 1971 he also hit his 500th home run, becoming the

ROBINSON
20

11th player in history to reach that total.

After the 1971 season, Robby was traded to the National League's Los Angeles Dodgers. The next year, the Dodgers traded him back to the American League to the California Angels.

Robinson was slowed by injuries in 1972 but returned to his old dangerous form in 1973. Most of the season he served as the Angels' designated hitter. He turned 38 during the season, yet hit 30 home runs, drove in 97 runs, and was walked 95 times — proof that with men on base, he still was one of the game's most feared batters.

At the end of the season, Robby could look back on 19 seasons and 2,579 games in the major leagues. He had come to bat 9,344 times, and baseball records listed these career statistics:

Avg.	R	H	2B	3B	HR	RBI	BB	SO
.287	1,724	2,783	496	69	552	1,710	1,308	1,410

Those figures assure Robinson of a prominent place in baseball history.

Frank has been called a top prospect to become the first black manager in the major leagues. By the spring of 1974, however, he was saying that he was "no longer seriously considering" such a possibility.

The majors didn't really want a black manager, Robinson believed. Frank had sought experience in running a team by managing the Santurce team in the Puerto Rican Winter League each year since 1966.

Meanwhile, he has said he expects to play at least 2 more years and continues to enjoy a pleasant, prosperous private life with his family in a Los Angeles suburb.

Robinson has been one of baseball's highest paid players for at least 15 years. He has earned more than $100,000 a year since 1966 and has saved a lot of it.

"I do old-fashioned things with my money now, like putting it in the bank," he said once, recalling his early years in Cincinnati when he squandered money as fast as he earned it.

He met his wife, Barbara, in 1961 and they were married that fall. The next year they adopted a son, Frank Kevin; and three years later their daughter, Nichelle, was born. Robinson was asked recently what his favorite recreation was. "Playing with my children," was his reply.

"I'm a simple, uncomplicated, single-minded kind of person," he said recently. "And my single-mindedness is baseball."

JACK NICKLAUS
BILL RUSSELL
MARK SPITZ
VINCE LOMBARDI
BILLIE JEAN KING
ROBERTO CLEMENTE
JOE NAMATH
BOBBY HULL
HANK AARON
JERRY WEST
TOM SEAVER
JACKIE ROBINSON
MUHAMMAD ALI
O. J. SIMPSON
JOHNNY BENCH
WILT CHAMBERLAIN
ARNOLD PALMER
A. J. FOYT
JOHNNY UNITAS
GORDIE HOWE

superstars!
superstars!
superstars!

CREATIVE EDUCATION SPORTS SUPERSTARS

WALT FRAZIER
PHIL AND TONY ESPOSITO
BOB GRIESE
FRANK ROBINSON
PANCHO GONZALES
LEE TREVINO
KAREEM ABDUL JABBAR
JEAN CLAUDE KILLY
EVONNE GOOLAGONG
ARTHUR ASHE
SECRETARIAT
ROGER STAUBACK
FRAN TARKENTON
BOBBY ORR
LARRY CSONKA
BILL WALTON
ALAN PAGE
PEGGY FLEMING
OLGA KORBUT
DON SCHULA
MICKEY MANTLE